A Dozen Dramatic Walks

in

Somerset

Simone Stanbrook–Byrne

and

James Clancy

CULM VALLEY PUBLISHING

Published by

Culm Valley Publishing Ltd
Culmcott House
Mill Street, Uffculme
Cullompton, Devon
EX15 3AT, UK
Tel: +44(0)1884 849085
Fax: +44(0)1884 840251
E-mail: info@culmvalleypublishing.co.uk
Website: www.culmvalleypublishing.co.uk

While every effort has been made to ensure the accuracy of the information contained in
this book, the publisher and authors accepts no liability for incorrect information
regarding public footpaths and rights of way. Neither Culm Valley Publishing Ltd nor
the authors shall be liable for any damages whatsoever arising in any way from the use of
or inability to use this book, or any material contained within it, or from any action or
decision taken as a result of using this book. Follow the country code.

First published 2011

ISBN 978-1-907942-02-0 paperback

British Library Cataloguing-in-Publication Data
A catalogue record for this book is available from the British Library

Typeset by Culm Valley Publishing Ltd
Printed and bound by T.J. International Ltd, Padstow, Cornwall
Front cover image: Cheddar Gorge © Simone Stanbrook-Byrne
Back cover image: Cow Castle, Simonsbath

Contents

Introduction

Writing this walking guide has been great fun. The authors have enjoyed the 'research' very much – the struggle to attain the highest points, route-finding on elusive paths, freezing conditions, fabulous views, pubs with open fires and the reward of ending the day where we intended.

By virtue of their nature 'dramatic walks' can involve challenging terrain so whenever you embark on a walk common sense must prevail: be properly shod and take care where you put your feet, be prepared for any kind of weather, take food and first aid supplies with you and make sure someone knows where you're going. Mobile phones are often useless in the middle of nowhere.

We also feel it's **imperative** that you take the **correct OS map** with you plus a **compass**, and are conversant with their use. Our sketch maps are precisely that – sketches – and are for rough guidance only and are not to scale.

You know you've had a good day's walking when you get home safely at the end of it and haven't been overtaken by the drama.

Useful websites:
A useful site which gives tips for moorland treks is: www.tourbytor.co.uk/equip_walk.php

Follow the countryside code:
www.naturalengland.org.uk/ourwork/enjoying/countrysidecode/default.aspx

Our grateful thanks to:
Brian and Jenny Willan;
David Shepherd;
Mike and Vanessa Brickman;
Nic and Ella, Tony and William.

Disclaimer

Points that should be borne in mind on any route – dramatic or not:

Public footpaths can be legally re-routed from the path shown on the map. In such cases they are usually clearly signposted. Where this has happened before the time of writing it has been noted in the text.

Most public footpaths are on private land. Please respect this.

Don't be surprised to find livestock grazing on public footpaths – and treat all animals with caution and respect.

If a field is planted with crops across a footpath, provision is usually made around the edge of the field.

Landmarks can change: trees and hedges may disappear; streams can dry up in warm weather; stiles turn into gates and vice versa; fences appear where previously there was no boundary. Even views are different as the seasons change. In such cases a modicum of common sense must be exercised – in conjunction with the map.

Public footpaths are at times blocked by barbed wire etc. Should this render the route impassable find the shortest detour around that section.

Please leave gates as you find them and if you have to climb them do so at the hinge end where it's stronger.

Exercise caution on wet stiles – they can be extremely slippery.

Take all your rubbish with you, don't damage anything during the walk and don't pick plants.

Keep your dogs under proper control.

We hope that you enjoy these walks without mishap, but urge you to exercise common sense at all times! Neither the authors nor Culm Valley Publishing Ltd. accepts responsibility for any misadventure which may occur during, or arise from, these walks and suggested routes.

Walk Locations

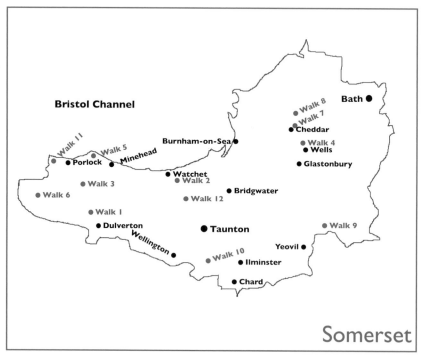

Walk 1	Winsford & the Punchbowl
Walk 2	West Quantoxhead & N Quantocks
Walk 3	Dunkery Beacon & the Draper's Way
Walk 4	Ebbor Gorge
Walk 5	Bossington
Walk 6	Simonsbath & the Barle Valley
Walk 7	Cheddar Gorge
Walk 8	Burrington Combe
Walk 9	Cadbury Castle & Corton Denham
Walk 10	Blagdon Hill
Walk 11	County Gate, Exmoor
Walk 12	Cothelstone & S Quantocks

Triscombe Stone (Walk 12)

Walk 1
Winsford & the Punchbowl

Winsford village is an idyllic spot, the confluence of the young River Exe and Winn Brook. The village has eight bridges spanning these rivers and a ford which can be quite exciting after wet weather. This is a walk of beautiful, contrasting and, at times, mysterious terrain which can be very damp underfoot in places so wellies are a good idea. We often see red deer on the moorland stretch of this walk.

Map: OS Outdoor Leisure 9, Exmoor 1:25 000

Start point: Village centre. Post code TA24 7JE. Grid ref SS905348

Directions to start: Winsford is just off the A396 Tiverton to Minehead road

Parking: There is an area for parking in the centre of the village

Distance: 5½ miles / 8.9km

Refreshments: Bridge Cottage Tea Gardens and Rooms: 01643 851362; The Royal Oak: 01643 851455

Toilets: Near the centre of the village along the lane from the parking area

Nearby places to stay: Halse Farm Camp Site: 01643 851259; Oaks Cottage B&B: 01643 851341; Karslake Country Guest House: 01643 851242

Nearby places of interest: Dunster Castle (NT): 01643 821314

Possible birds include: Blue tit, buzzard, carrion crow, collared dove, dunnock, grey wagtail, nuthatch, pheasant, robin, rook, woodpigeon

Authors' tip: This walk is full of views but if time and energy permit you may wish to walk / drive to the viewpoint shown on the OS map at grid ref SS878341 which is on the lane so easy to find. Additionally, the Caratacus Stone can also be visited by walking further along the lane from Folly, about ¼ mile beyond the footpath turning (grid ref SS889335). Look out for the shelter which protects it. The inscription says 'CARAACI NEPUS' which means 'kinsman of Caratacus' who led the Britons against the Romans. The earliest documentation of the stone was in 1219. Spellings of the name vary

Note: Be aware: part of this route is across open moorland, so a map and compass are needed – and clear weather conditions

---

Leave the village centre along the lane signposted for Withypool, South Molton and Tarr Steps and after a few metres, at the war memorial, go right off this lane through the ford (or over the little bridge). You've passed the Bridge Cottage Tea Gardens & Rooms on your right and after the ford continue ahead on the lane. There

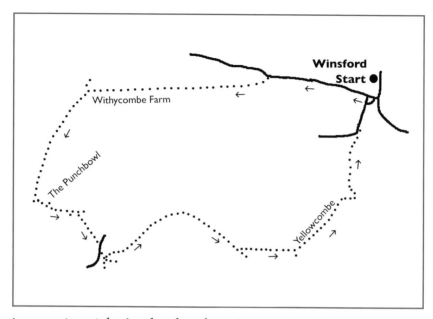

is a turning right for the church and a couple of footpaths on the right, all of which you ignore. The lane climbs gently and as the houses lessen you come to a footpath left off the lane through a gate, about 0.3 miles from the village centre, signposted to Winsford Hill via Punchbowl. Take this.

A few metres beyond the gate off the lane you see a stile on the right leading to a narrow path. Follow this path with gardens to your right and to your left a boundary with glorious views beyond towards wooded hillsides. The path leads into a field across which you head in the same direction as before with the fence to your left and the valley sloping down to your left. Winn Brook is the river running through here. Yellow markers show that you are on the right line.

Follow these yellow markers through successive fields in a fairly constant direction and eventually the buildings of Withycombe Farm come into view. Just before you reach the farm there is a short, well-signed footpath diversion taking you slightly right, but the yellow waymarkers are clear so keep following them until they lead you to the tarmac farm drive. Here turn left to join a blue waymarked bridleway which runs along this drive, the fingerpost shows that you are heading for Winsford Hill ¾ mile away.

Follow the drive as it passes the buildings of Withycombe Farm on your left. Before you reach a large wooden barn ahead look out for the blue marker painted on a stone barn wall on your left. Here turn 90° left to pass between the stone barn and the wooden barn, following the track which crosses the stream on a small bridge. Beyond the bridge look out for the blue arrow on a tree trunk directing you to bear right uphill along a track. Follow this, the hedge to your left and the final farm buildings now down to your right. Within 100m of the bridge the track bends left to pass through another gate. Immediately after this turn right and head uphill through the field, the fence on your right. There is a good view here, ahead and left, into the Punchbowl.

Sunbeams over Winn Brook

Looking into the Punchbowl

The trudge uphill is eased by pausing to enjoy superb views as you ascend this field. Near the top of the field you pass an old treed boundary heading left down the slope. Just after here pass through the gate on your right then turn left to continue uphill as before, now with the boundary on your left. Another blue fingerpost directs you here. This leads to a gate onto open moorland. A well-trodden, grassy path beyond this continues ahead. Follow it. As you ascend views of the Punchbowl open up to your left. Also spare a glance behind from time to time as the vista is thirst-quenching and Dunkery Beacon with its cairn, the highest point on Exmoor, is clearly seen. On a clear day the coast of Wales beyond the Bristol Channel is also visible. Being out of breath is well-rewarded by these view-stops.

Stay on this lovely path with its occasional stubby trees as it bears left round the head of the Punchbowl. It gets quite close to the edge so be cautious. As the path rounds the Punchbowl you will occasionally see moorland paths coming in from the right but continue ahead with the Punchbowl down to your left.

As you start to go down the far side of the Punchbowl you will see a fork in the path (grid ref SS881341) the left hand option hugging the rim of the 'bowl' and the right hand option heading across the moorland of Winsford Hill which is all National Trust land. Take the right hand fork, a lovely, broad grassy path. About 500m from the fork the path gets slightly worn and then broadens out into a meeting of ways (grid ref SS887342). Two paths lead on, more or less ahead, a third goes to the right (south east) and a fourth goes right back on yourself. Take the third, south easterly path heading right. This soon leads to a lane where a house called Folly is ahead of you. Turn right along the lane for a very short distance until you see a footpath and bridleway sign left off the lane. The footpath sign states that Winsford via Yellowcombe is 2½ miles. About 100m from this sign you see a gate on the left which now tells you that Winsford via Yellowcombe is 1½ miles – the quickest mile on Exmoor you will ever walk.

You are now going to follow the footpath rather than the bridleway, so go through this gate and ahead on the footpath, as shown by the fingerpost, forking left very soon to follow the path down towards the stream and beneath trees. This is a delightful stretch of walking with ancient mossy trees and little waterfalls, a very different terrain and atmosphere to the airy heights around the Punchbowl. It feels very ancient down here.

The buildings of Halse Farm appear on the hillside ahead, across the stream. Follow the path with the rushy water to your left – it may be less rushy in dry summers but when we walked this in the deep, white frost of midwinter it was like walking through a dreamscape. Occasional footpath markers indicate that you are on the right path through the woods. Beyond Halse Farm the path

The Punchbowl and Exmoor's red deer
Legend has it that the Punchbowl was created by the devil scooping out a well, the discarded earth being thrown over his shoulder to make Dunkery Hill. A less romantic, and possibly more likely, explanation is that it was formed by glacial action during the last ice age. The area abounds with wildlife and red deer, our largest wild mammal, can often be seen. They have inhabited Exmoor since prehistoric times. With luck you will see a mature stag with full antlers – these are shed every year and re-grow in the spring.

crosses a stream (again this may be dry in summer) and continues ahead as before. Soon a three-way fingerpost shows a bridleway coming in from the right, the distance on the sign here is of dubious accuracy but keep ahead in the same direction as before, now on the bridleway.

Eventually you cross the stream and continue with it on your right. You reach the astonishingly isolated Yellowcombe Cottages, home in the late 19thC to the ancestors of one of our friends. The 1901 census shows that the Upham and Vaulter families lived in these two cottages and in 1841 Fanny Upham's grandparents, Richard and Isabella Gunter were in residence.

Beyond the cottage the bridleway splits. Don't go right over a stile here but continue ahead through a gate to join a path, the stream departs right and you leave it and the cottages behind. Follow the clear path with the valley down to your right, ignoring any lefts or rights. Eventually you see Winsford ahead in the valley. Here the path bends left and becomes stony and slippery. Take care. Soon you see the houses of the village outskirts and you meet the road. Turn right along the road back to the village centre.

Walk 2

West Quantoxhead & the North Quantocks

This is a walk of wonderful combes and airy heights with some idyllic spots for picnics when you reach Smith's Combe. Apart from the climb out of Smith's Combe there are no serious ascents, the first climb on The Great Road being steady rather than steep. There is a chance of seeing red deer.

Map: OS Explorer 140 Quantock Hills and Bridgwater 1:25 000

Start point: National Trust car park near Beacon Hill. No post code. Grid ref: ST116410

Directions to start: West Quantoxhead is on the A39. Turn into the village and at the Staple Cross junction turn up Hill Lane. Go over the cattle grid and continue on the dirt track to the car park

Parking: In the car park at the bottom of Beacon Hill, as above

Distance: 4½ miles / 7.2km

Refreshments: Hood Arms, Kilve: 01278 741210; tea rooms and gardens in East Quantoxhead; The Windmill Bar and Restaurant, West Quantoxhead: 01984 633004

Toilets: None en route

Nearby places to stay: Hood Arms, Kilve: 01278 741210; Stilegate, West Quantoxhead: 01984 639119

Nearby places of interest: West Somerset Railway: 01643 704996

Possible birds include: Blackbird, carrion crow, lesser redpoll, raven, robin, siskin, stonechat

Authors' tip: The delightful tea rooms and gardens in East Quantoxhead are well worth a visit. Part of a private cottage, it's a case of turning up and walking in to find someone but this slightly quirky approach adds to the charm of chintz and pretty garden. We were there on a freezing cold day at the beginning of March and the hot chocolate and toast were exceedingly welcome

Note: Be aware: part of this route is across open moorland, so a map and compass are needed – and clear weather conditions

---

When you arrive in this car park you are met with superb views south over Weacombe Combe and up to Weacombe Hill beyond. Start the walk by the stone plinth showing the National Trust symbol and indicating that you are in the area of Beacon Hill.

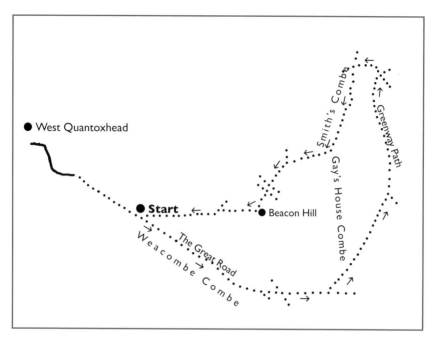

There is an information board attached. Just to the left of this plinth there is a clear track heading in a south-easterly direction up onto the hill. This track is called The Great Road. Follow it.

As you climb pause to glance around as the views open up, over your right shoulder are the Brendon Hills and behind you is the sea and coastline around Minehead. Ignore any paths left or right and keep on this track until, after about ¾ mile from the car park, you see a track going right. Ignore it and also ignore the one soon after on the left. You then reach a staggered crossways of tracks, the one on the left going obliquely back (grid ref ST127406). The way lies straight ahead, (although it's worth a short detour to the right in order to get the view down Weacombe Combe from its head).

Continue ahead on The Great Road – you will eventually see the looming bulk of Hinkley Point in the very far distance to your left.

More picturesquely you will pass the head of Gay's House Combe down to the left of the track. Keep a sharp eye out and just after this combe, at grid ref ST132406, look out for a track across the grass to the left. Leave The Great Road and take this track, which skirts the top of Gay's House Combe heading just east of north. This is a lovely path with views across the combe to the left and to the coastline ahead of you. The views on the right eventually open out too, to the villages of Kilve and Stogursey and, eventually, East Quantoxhead. Also, in the distance, you might see traffic on the A39.

Gay's House Combe on the left runs into Smith's Combe – keep ahead on the clear track above them until it descends to a fingerpost at grid ref ST133422. Here turn left towards Perry on the Coleridge Way (see feature on page 17), denoted by a quill on the post (this is also part of the Quantock Greenway). The path drops down to a fingerpost at Smith's Combe. The Coleridge Way

Weacombe Combe

Smith's Combe

towards Perry continues ahead here across a series of little footbridges. Cross just one of these and then turn left into the delightful Smith's Combe with its beautiful trees and sparkling spring. This is a real treat after the airy heights you've been walking previously – it is an idyllic place to relax and picnic by the stream. You are greeted by a quaint little waterfall aside a splendid old tree. Admire the area and then continue inland along the main path to explore the combe further. As you wend your way along you pass several mossy trees and cross the stream several times.

After a final crossing of the stream the path begins to ascend and you skirt the edge of a coniferous woodland leaving Smith's Combe behind you. You are soon passing majestic pine trees on your left (we saw lesser redpolls here high in the treetops). Keep climbing and, as the trees to your left drop away, pause to look back through the combe to the coastline before continuing uphill along this clear path. You are walking between two areas of rising ground. When a track comes down from the right to meet you ignore this and continue.

The path rises to a broad crossing track. Continue ahead here to a visible post 75m beyond at an even broader crossing track. Once the post is reached you will see it indicates that Bicknoller Post is to your left and Perry to your right. The post is located at grid ref ST124412. Beyond the post and crossing path bear left on the well trodden track opposite – you are now heading for the trig point at the summit of Beacon Hill which should be seen ahead.

Once at the trig point you are standing at 310m above sea level and the 360° views afforded from this elevated position are fantastic. On a clear day you can look north across the Bristol Channel to

The Quantocks

In 1956 the diverse and beautiful Quantock Hills were the first area of England to be designated an Area of Outstanding Natural Beauty but the region hasn't always been a place of peace and tranquility. The nearby coastal town of Watchet suffered unwanted attention from the Vikings during the 10thC and the Hills also  saw activity during the English Civil War when the Royalist stronghold of Dunster Castle was under siege. Later in the 17thC, when the Monmouth Rebellion came to an end, many of the Duke's supporters were executed around here – some being hanged on Cothelstone Hill. The Quantocks have been occupied since prehistoric times, archaeological finds such as Mesolithic flints, Bronze-Age barrows and Roman coins, indicating successive populations. The Quantocks offer many miles of good walking, including the 36 mile Coleridge Way, named for Samuel Taylor Coleridge who lived at Nether Stowey for 3 years in the late 18thC. The name 'Quantocks' means 'settlement by a circle of hills', Cantuc being Celtic for 'rim' or 'circle'.

Wales. The Brendon Hills are prominent to the west with Exmoor beyond. The Mendips can be seen to the east and the Blackdowns to the south. You'll also notice a diminutive cairn close by and beyond, in the same direction, is the car park from whence you started which nestles in front of the Staple Plantation woodland.

From the trig point head for the downhill path just left of the cairn, which heads west from here. There are fantastic views as you descend to meet a broad track. Turn left along here with Vinny Combe to your right and follow this path to the car park.

Majestic pine trees

Pandora graces Weacombe Combe

Dunkery Beacon & the Draper's Way

Although Dunkery Beacon is one of the English Marilyns (see feature on page 79) and is the most elevated point in southern England outside Dartmoor, you are starting this walk at quite a high point so, although not entirely flat, there aren't any really dreadful ascents. It is a walk of stunning views and fabulous open spaces and is particularly lovely when the heather is in bloom. You have a good chance of seeing red deer (see feature on page 12).

Map: OS Outdoor Leisure 9, Exmoor 1:25 000

Start point: Dunkery Bridge. No post code. Grid ref SS895406

Directions to start: Dunkery Bridge is on the road to Luccombe, signed off the B3224, Wheddon Cross to Exford road

Parking: There is a car park at Dunkery Bridge, clearly shown on the OS map

Distance: 5½ / 8.9km or longer option 7½ miles / 12.1km

Refreshments: Horner Tea Gardens, Horner is 4 miles away: 01643 862380; The Rest and be Thankful Inn, Wheddon Cross is 2½ miles away: 01643 841222

Toilets: None en route, the nearest are at Horner village 4 miles away

Nearby places to stay: The Rest and be Thankful Inn, Wheddon Cross: 01643 841222

Nearby places of interest: Selworthy village (see feature on page 38)

Possible birds include: Bullfinch, carrion crow, house sparrow, jackdaw, magpie, meadow pipit, raven, skylark, starling, yellowhammer

Authors' tip: Wrap up well for this walk as it's always windy at the Beacon! Although there are options for shorter routes the full distance is highly recommended

Note: Be aware: part of this route is across open moorland, so a map and compass are needed – and clear weather conditions

---

From the car park cross the road and take the bridleway signposted Exford 5 miles. Follow this track across the moor with rising ground away to your right and sweeping views to your left. Keep on this for 1¼ miles until you reach an acute right turn off this path heading back up towards the cairn of Dunkery Beacon. Take this. Your ascent is well rewarded with a spectacular 360°

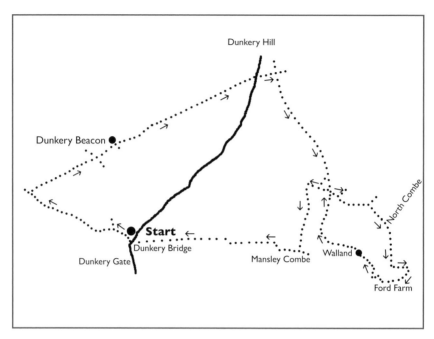

panorama at the summit. From here you overlook Exmoor to the south and west and the Brendon and Quantock Hills to the east. There are glimpses of the Exmoor coastline to the north and on a clear day Wales can be seen beyond the Bristol Channel. Not only is this a spectacular place to be but at 519m you can also claim the distinction of being the highest person in Somerset. Before you leave take a few moments to study the nearby stone plinth on which a board indicates with arrows and distances what you've been looking at in every direction.

From the cairn continue in the same direction as before taking the path ahead which leads to a lane in just under a mile. Don't take the path heading right from the cairn (south east) unless you would like a swift return to your car.

Once you reach the lane you'll be greeted by a bridleway fingerpost (in inclement weather you may wish to note that your car is right along this lane). Cross the road and follow the bridleway signed to Brockwell 1¼ miles. You're not going to Brockwell, but this is your direction for approx 400m at which point seek out a pile of stones signifying the right hand turn you need off this bridleway (grid ref SS906422). When you find the stones turn right down this narrower path ignoring any lefts and rights until, just before you reach a hedge boundary, you come across a four-way fingerpost.

Here you have an option. For those on the shorter walk take a right signed to Draper's Way 1½ miles and follow the path, boundary to your left, to a three-way fingerpost directing you on for Mansley Combe. Then continue from (*) below. For those on the longer route (highly recommended) proceed straight ahead at the four-way post signed to Wootton Courtney. About 100m beyond here you will see a small bridleway gate next to a metal farm gate. There

View from Dunkery Beacon

Across the valley to Little Quarme Wood & Blagdon Wood

are blue arrows signed to Wootton Courtney left and Draper's Way right. Go through the gate leaving the moorland behind you and follow the right hand boundary of this field.

Continue through a second field keeping the boundary on your right. You then reach a further gate with a blue bridleway marker and a signpost. Go right here on the bridleway signposted for Draper's Way. Another wooden farm gate awaits directly opposite. Go through this (not the gate on the left) and keep ahead down the field with beautiful valley views across to Little Quarme and Blagdon Woods. Initially further blue blobs on the left-hand fence encourage you along your route but these soon peter out. Keep descending with the fence on your left.

At the bottom you'll reach a shed with a corrugated iron roof and next to this you'll find another fence and gate with a blue blob. Beyond this gate and the shed, walk ahead through a churned up area for a few metres until you see blue squares on tree trunks to your right which guide you through another gate. Beyond here bear slightly right and then continue along a lovely sunken path running beneath trees along the bottom of the field. Blue markers still direct you.

Emerge from the sunken path and you will see more markers directing you ahead, along the bottom of the field, with the fence on your right. At the end there is a gate, go through and turn right to another gate about 50m away. Go through here and look out for the blue arrow on the holly tree to your right. Continue as directed straight down the next field with the boundary on your right, passing a pollarded tree with a marker and 150m further you will find a fingerpost.

Follow the direction which says 'permitted bridleway Wheddon Cross avoiding farmyard'. This leads to a gate behind the house of Ford Farm and to a track which then leads to another gate. Beyond this gate you find a farm drive. There is a three-way fingerpost here, turn right in the direction of Dunkery via Spangate along the tarmac drive, bending right with it as it goes up to approach Walland Farm. Just before the gate of Walland Farm turn

Dunkery Beacon

Dunkery Beacon, as part of the Holnicote Estate, was given to the National Trust in 1935 by Sir Thomas Acland, Colonel Wiggin and Allan Hughes. It is part of a designated SSSI and you will notice bronze-age burial mounds around the area. The summit is dominated by a massive stone cairn. Cairns are man-made features and nowadays are generally used as a landmark. Their original uses were as waymarkers or memorials and smaller cairns can be found throughout moorland areas.

Dunkery sunset

left along the track and follow it up into the field. It loops round to another gate, join the track beyond this and continue uphill. This track winds up to the buildings of North Hill, just under ½ mile from Walland. Although this track up from Ford Farm isn't shown as a public right of way on the map, the blue signs indicate that this is now a permitted bridleway.

Beyond North Hill continue on the track behind the buildings to two gates, the left-hand one of which has blue markers. Go through this and continue up the track (ignoring track to left) with the field boundary to your right. This leads to another gate and then through a second field to yet another gate and three-way fingerpost. Turn left here towards Mansley Combe. (*) It is at this point that those on the longer route are rejoining the shorter option.

Follow the path with the boundary wall and lovely views to your left. As the boundary takes a sharp left go left with it and continue downhill, still keeping it on your left. A sign shows that you are heading in the direction of Wheddon Cross. The track eventually leads you down to a gate barring your way. Go through and bear slightly right on the main path, still downhill. This path is lovely when the rhododendrons are in flower, but is quite sticky walking underfoot after wet weather. At a crossing of paths go right – you will see an arrow on a post for guidance. The River Avill can be heard away to your left. When the path meets the river cross it (this was just manageable in walking boots in mid-winter!) and beyond the river continue right uphill on the path signed on the fingerpost for Dunkery Gate.

The path emerges from the trees. Continue in the open and soon you will have a boundary on your right and the valley below to the left. The track passes through a field boundary to then continue in the same direction. At the end of this field turn right through a bridleway gate and continue up the next field for 75m, river to your left. You reach a post at which you turn left. The track leads clearly for nearly ½ mile to a final gate beyond which you will see the car park.

Evening stags near Dunkery Beacon

Ebbor Gorge

This less well-known gorge is much smaller than that at Cheddar (Walk 7) and has a wonderful, secretive feel to it. Glorious scenery and vast views await you above it and if you take the option to also explore within its depths you will enjoy the gorge's rather 'lost world' quality. Stout footwear is essential, as always, and there are the inevitable ups and downs which go with this kind of terrain. Depending on the option you choose, this route can be quite adventurous. At the time of writing the stiles on this route weren't dog-friendly.

Map: OS Explorer 141 Cheddar Gorge and Mendip Hills West   1:25 000

Start point: Ebbor Gorge car park. No post code. Grid ref ST520485

Directions to start: Ebbor Gorge is on the road from Priddy heading towards Wells, just under 3 miles from Priddy

Parking: There is a National Nature Reserve car park just off the road

Distance: 6 miles / 9.6km + optional exploration within the gorge which could add up to 1½ miles / 2.4km

Refreshments: Priddy has two pubs – The New Inn: 01749 676465 and the Queen Victoria: 01749 676385

Toilets: None en route

Nearby places to stay: The New Inn: 01749 676465; Cheddar Camping and Caravanning Club Site: 01749 870241

Nearby places of interest: Wookey Hole: 01749 672243

Possible birds include: Blackbird, blue tit, buzzard, carrion crow, chaffinch, goldfinch, great spotted woodpecker, great tit, green woodpecker, house sparrow, jay, kestrel, magpie, nuthatch, pheasant, raven, robin, rook, song thrush, sparrowhawk, starling, tawny owl, woodpigeon

Authors' tip: Although the path through the bottom of the gorge is not necessarily part of the route we recommend a detour into this fascinating area. You can decide how far along it you wish to explore but the more adventurous can go right the way through to ascend at the narrow, craggy end, re-joining the path to the airy viewpoint if you wish. To descend down the gorge is treacherous!

From the car park first admire the view of Glastonbury Tor to the south. This is a good start. Beyond the north-west end of the car park you will find a little shelter housing information boards about

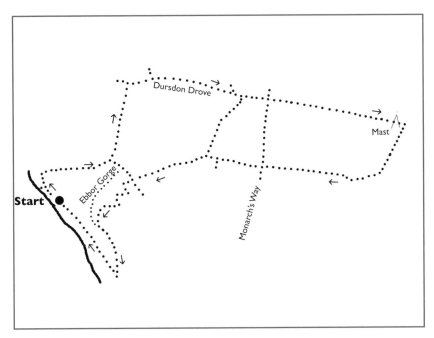

the area. From here two paths lead off, follow the one which goes away to the right and soon leads you to a good viewing point over the gorge. Continue ahead beyond here ignoring paths joining from the left. The path bends right and when you reach a stile cross it and go left uphill. A few metres up and you will find another arrow directing you right along the path. This is a bit of a clamber which can be sticky underfoot. At the top of the steep bit you find another yellow-arrowed post which points you straight across the field ahead. At the top of the field you will find an arrow on a diminutive post telling you to bear right through the trees on a well-trodden path.

Emerge from the trees and walk straight ahead to a stile in the far boundary. Ignore the path to the right in front of the stile which goes into trees, cross the stile and bear right as directed by the arrow attached to it. You are crossing the bottom of a field to the far boundary with the trees of Ebbor Wood down to your right.

Go through the next boundary to follow the clear path beyond which eventually curves left to meet a stone wall and another stile. Cross the stile and continue on the path across the bottom of the next field.

At the end of the field you see a path coming up out of the woods on your right. Ignore this and cross the stile ahead of you, staying out of the trees. Beyond here bear left as directed by the arrow up to a boundary with a rather tired stile. Keep straight ahead after this enjoying the surrounding views and at the end of this field negotiate the obstacle of stile and wall, then head across the next field. The end of Ebbor Wood is still down to your right and as you cross the field you will see a cairn away to your right in the next field.

At the end of the field the path reaches a stile. Cross this and turn right along the broad track – this is Dursdon Drove with its lovely,

Admiring the clifftop views over Ebbor Gorge

The path through the gorge

ancient boundary walls – you now have nearly 1½ miles of its company, a level stretch of walking and part of the West Mendip Way. Eventually you see the buildings of Higher Pitts Farm off to your right. Keep straight ahead ignoring a bridleway left. About 30m beyond this the track, together with the West Mendip Way, swings right towards the farm and Wookey Hole but ignore this and keep ahead here in the same direction as before, away from the farm.

You stay with Dursdon Drove all the way to a mast, as you approach this look left to make out a tumulus in the field. About 20m beyond the mast turn right in front of a house along the private road to Rookham View which is a public footpath. After about 100m ignore the footpath left and continue, passing the house on the left which enjoys amazing views. The track swings right over a cattle grid after which you leave it to veer left, as shown by the fingerpost, to cross the field towards some trees.

These trees surround farm buildings. Walk round the end of the trees to a gate in the wall. Go through here, admiring still more big views away to your left over the city of Wells, England's smallest city, and the surrounding countryside. Beyond the gate walk up the field, as shown by the arrow on the gate, to a stile. Cross this and walk through the next field to another stile in the far boundary and beyond here keep ahead in the same line through the next field with the fence on your right. Pause to look behind you to the left where you can make out Wells Cathedral.

At the end of the field the Monarch's Way crosses at right angles but this isn't for us (it was the escape route taken by Charles II in 1651 after the Battle of Worcester) so pass through the boundary and go straight on as before with the fence still on your right. You reach another stile with an arrow (ignore the green lane going off left), cross the stile and continue ahead up the next field with a hedge on your right. At the top of the field go left without passing through the gate to walk beside the fence, keeping it to your right. You are now on the West Mendip Way again. Soon you find yourself re-entering the Ebbor Gorge Nature Reserve. Follow the well-trodden path downhill towards the gorge.

Cross a stile into trees, the ground drops away to your right into the wooded gorge, and at a crossing of ways keep ahead, signed for cliff and car park. (*) Remember this spot, as those who wish to explore into the gorge later can rejoin this path for a second time if they decide to do a full, additional loop. At the next waymarker keep ahead towards the cliff which you will reach in a few metres. Go carefully as you approach, the panorama is stunning, the drop would be more than stunning if you went over the edge.

Drink your fill of the view then return the few metres to the waymarker which now directs you right for the car park. Descend the steps and at the bottom turn right towards the car park. In

Ebbor Gorge & Wookey Hole
The limestone Ebbor Gorge in the Mendip Hills is an excellent, woodland wildlife habitat with a diversity of flora and fauna. It is home to both lesser and greater horseshoe bats and a variety of butterflies. There has been much debate over the formation of gorges in this area, the 'collapsed cave' theory being popular during the 19thC. Current thinking says that Ebbor Gorge was formed by erosion during the ice-age when 'summer' melt-water gouged it out. Eventually, as the land thawed and underground drainage and caves developed, the eroding waterways disappeared, leaving the gorges dry. The area was once mined for limestone, coal, iron and lead and during these operations the remains of ice-age mammals were discovered including hippopotamus and straight-tusked elephants. These now reside in the Wells and Mendip Museum. Wookey Hole was formed by the action of the River Axe and 50,000 years ago was considered by our ancestors as a safe and relatively comfortable place to live.

about 20m you reach a right turn which takes you into the gorge. Here you have an option.

Those planning to explore this bird-rich and beautiful place can enter the gorge along this path, exploring as far in as you wish. Don't be tempted to go left or right up the scree slopes, but you can go through the gorge as it narrows, climbing the steep and rocky ascent to a crossing path. Exploration of the narrow part of the ravine is quite challenging, and descending down it is not to be recommended, so only go in (or up) as far as suits you. If you go all the way to the crossing path beyond the rocky ravine turn right (an arrow directs) and after a few metres right again and you will find yourself back at (*) above, following signs back to the car park. To do this complete loop would add just over a mile to your distance.

Those who aren't going into the gorge, or who have done that and have now returned to this point at the entrance to the gorge, should continue in the direction signed for the car park. At the time of writing this took you past a big brown bear watching over the path – he's nine feet tall and made of willow, you can't miss him. Long may he survive!

The path leads up to a cross path along which you go left, still clearly signed for the car park. You leave the reserve through a kissing gate, beyond which you see another waymarker directing you right for the cars. Follow this, passing the memorial stone which shows that this area was donated to the National Trust in memory of Winston Churchill. From here you can look across to the cliff on the other side of the gorge where you were standing earlier. It's a short walk from this memorial to your car.

Ebbor Bear

Waterfall (County Gate, Exmoor)

Above the Punchbowl (Winsford & the Punchbowl)

In Mansley Combe (Dunkery Beacon)

Smith's Combe (West Quantoxhead)   *Towards Mansley Combe (Dunkery Beacon)*

Cliff view (Ebbor Gorge)

Bossington Hill and Exmoor coast (Bossington)

Goats (Burrington Combe)

View of Blackdowns (Blagdon Hill)

Morning frost above the Barle Valley (Simonsbath)

View from Lydeard Hill (Cothelstone)

Trig point at Will's Neck (Cothelstone)

Glee on the ramparts (Cadbury Castle)

Landacre Bridge (Simonsbath)

Through the gorge (Ebbor Gorge)

View across Glenthorne Estate (County Gate, Exmoor)

The Gorge (Cheddar Gorge)

Walk 5

Bossington

The first part of this walk is through the National Trust woodlands above Allerford and Selworthy while the latter stretch is very high and open along the delightful grassy paths which traverse Selworthy Beacon and Bossington Hill. Although there is inevitably some ascent to gain this height the terrain underfoot is mostly good and not excessively swampy.

Map: OS Outdoor Leisure 9, Exmoor 1:25 000

Start point: Bossington car park. Post code TA24 8HQ. Grid ref SS897480

Directions to start: Bossington is accessed off the A39 at Allerford

Parking: There is a National Trust car park at Bossington

Distance: 5½ miles / 8.9km

Refreshments: Kitnor's Tea Rooms and Gardens: 01643 862643; Periwinkle Tea Rooms and Gardens, Selworthy: 01643 862769

Toilets: In the car park at Bossington

Nearby places to stay: Tudor Cottage: 01643 862255

Nearby places of interest: Dunster Castle (NT): 01643 821314

Possible birds include: Buzzard, carrion crow, great tit, green woodpecker, grey heron, jay, peregrine, pheasant, raven, red-legged partridge, song thrush, stonechat, woodpigeon

Authors' tip: Although the route doesn't pass through them it is well worth finding time to visit both Allerford with its ancient packhorse bridge and the idyllic, copiously thatched, National Trust village of Selworthy

Note: Be aware: part of this route is across open moorland, so a map and compass are needed – and clear weather conditions

Leave the car park across the footbridge opposite the toilets. This busy little river is Horner Water. Beyond the bridge take the footpath signed to the right for Lynch and Selworthy. In about 30m turn right through the kissing gate and follow the path as it winds above Horner Water, down to your right. Ascend some steps, go through another gate to enter a field and continue with the fence on your right.

After about 50m turn right towards Selworthy, as a fingerpost directs, to enter another field and walk straight ahead to the far

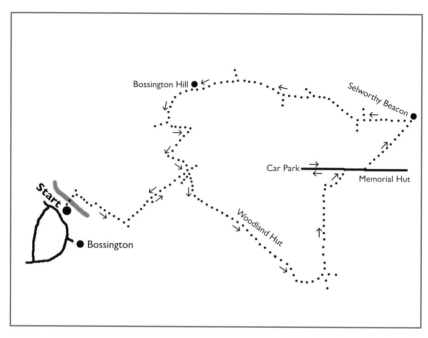

boundary. There are lovely views to the right now towards the combes and heights of Exmoor and Dunkery Beacon can be seen. At the far boundary pass through a gate and turn left on the bridleway to Selworthy Beacon. Soon the path leads you through a gate into Allerford Woods. Continue beyond here on a broad path up through the woodland, noting the old dry stone wall which the Trust has recently restored. It is thought this could be around 200 years old. At a four-way fingerpost keep ahead in the direction of Selworthy Beacon, 1¼ miles. Minehead is also in this direction. When you pause for breath glance back at the high moorland views behind.

As you climb a wall joins you on the right and when this wall bends right you will find a small gate in it. (If you miss this, in a few metres you find a four-way fingerpost none of whose options mention Selworthy, so if you reach this post go back and find the gate.) Go right through the gate and beyond it you will find a fingerpost with two options. St. Agnes Fountain, Allerford and Bossington are down in roughly the direction from which you have come, but the option you need is the narrow path going left uphill through the trees, signed towards Selworthy Cross.

The narrow path ascends to meet a broad crossing path along which you turn right. This is a lovely stretch of walking with good views to the right if you can glimpse them through the trees. At a crossing path keep straight on and you reach a very 'organic' wooden hut with benches – handy for a picnic. Keep on this main track, ignoring any lefts, rights or crossing paths, until it drops to meet a crossing of ways with fingerposts which show that you have come from the direction of Hurlstone and Bossington, Allerford is right and Selworthy straight on. Our route goes left, uphill, on the bridleway signed to Selworthy Beacon (the energetic amongst you have the option to visit the other villages on foot, but Selworthy Beacon is where you are aiming after doing so).

Bossington Hill and the Exmoor Coast

You meet another fingerpost which indicates that you are walking up through Holnicote Combe. As you pause for breath by this post you are at 181m. Keep straight on up to the Beacon which is 308m above sea level and one of the English Marilyns (see feature on page 79). At a gate admire the beautiful construction of the mossy wall which you're passing through and continue uphill. Another fingerpost shows that you have ½ mile still to go to the Beacon.

The path emerges from the trees and you reach a bench with excellent views. Pass the bench on your left (or have a rest if you prefer) and follow the path which bears right on its way to the top. Keep ahead, uphill on this path until you reach a lane, about 400m from the bench.

It's worth a brief diversion of 300m here to a fabulous viewpoint, so go left along this lane which ends at a stunning view over Porlock Bay. This is the National Trust land of Bossington Hill, the actual hill is away to your right, above the bay and you'll be up there soon. After absorbing all this retrace your steps to the point at which you joined the lane and continue along it for another 200m. Here, just right off the lane, you will find the rather grand memorial hut erected in memory of Sir Thomas Dyke Acland who died in 1871. His descendants subsequently donated this estate to the Trust. Back at the lane you will find a fingerpost directing you across the lane away from the hut and up onto the Beacon, follow this lovely, clear path with thirst-quenching views until you reach the cairn and trig point.

The path you need from here is the one which goes sharp left just before the cairn, heading west. Head along here on this clear path and in 400m you will be joined by the South West Coast Path. Keep ahead in the same direction, now on the coast path, and eventually you are rewarded with astonishing coastal views. Relish them.

Five hundred metres after joining the coast path you reach a fingerpost at grid ref SS910482 where there is an option to go left off the coast path towards Lynch Combe. Take this and you reach a fingerpost at which you now ignore the left option to Bossington via Lynch but instead keep straight on towards the summit of Bossington Hill. At the next clear fork go left uphill and at the top of the hill you find a cairn and more stunning views.

Pass the cairn on your right and leave the hill on the path which veers left in a south westerly direction. This starts to drop steeply, the village which you can see ahead way below you is Porlock, the coast is ahead to your right. The village of Allerford can be seen to your left below the woodland and soon Bossington comes into view, tucked down below the hill and closer than Porlock. The path drops down to a bench at which you turn left along a slightly wider path which winds around Bossington Hill, which rises steeply to the left. The path starts to drop and eventually bends

The descent from Bossington Hill into the Vale of Porlock

Selworthy

This quintessential English village is part of the National Trust's Holnicote Estate which belonged to the Acland family until 1944. Very few buildings in the village pre-date 1828, when the philanthropic Sir Thomas Acland rebuilt the village to accommodate aged estate residents. The very noticeable white-washed All Saints' Church dates from the 15thC with an older tower. Bury Castle is a Roman encampment to the north of the village. In the Domesday Book Selworthy is referred to as Selewrda, the name means something along the lines of ' a settlement near willow trees'. The Holnicote Estate is one of the largest owned by the Trust and extends to around 12,500 acres (over 5,000 hectares).

right to continue into woodland. Another lovely stretch of dry stone wall appears to the right and you eventually reach a four-way fingerpost which you may recognize from earlier. Turn right here towards Bossington on the bridleway, heading downhill with moorland views ahead of you and a stone wall on your left. You are now retracing your steps, but in reverse it is a different walk!

At the next fingerpost keep on down the bridleway towards Lynch and eventually pass through the gate leaving Allerford Woods. Continue down the path which drops to meet a crossing path. Turn right on the yellow-marked footpath towards Bossington, walking through one field, at the end of which turn left (ignoring the well-trodden path ahead) to follow the fence on your left. This quickly leads you to the steps down towards the river. Turn right at the bottom of the steps and follow this path back to the bridge into the car park.

Walk 6
Simonsbath & the Barle Valley

This is another route of great contrasts, airy open moorland and idyllic river valleys, beech woodland and field paths. Add to this a good smattering of historic sites and the chance of seeing wild red deer and Exmoor ponies, and you have a classic walk which has been one of our favourites for many years.

Map: OS Outdoor Leisure 9, Exmoor 1:25 000

Start point: Village centre. Post code TA24 7SH. Grid ref SS774394

Directions to start: Simonsbath is on the junction of the B3358 and B3223, south of Lynton and Lynmouth

Parking: Exmoor National Park car park, signed off the main road. There is an honesty box here

Distance: 7½ miles / 12km

Refreshments: Boevey's Tea Rooms: 01643 831622; The Exmoor Forest Inn: 01643 831341

Toilets: In the car park

Nearby places to stay: Simonsbath House Hotel: 01643 831259; The Exmoor Forest Inn: 01643 831341

Nearby places of interest: Tarr Steps Woodland Nature Reserve: 01398 323841; Watersmeet (NT): 01598 753348

Possible birds include: Blackbird, blue tit, buzzard, carrion crow, magpie, pheasant, raven, robin, rook, starling, stonechat

Authors' tip: You have a very good chance of seeing Exmoor ponies on this walk. The pure-bred Exmoor is Britain's oldest native breed and has its own Society to help preserve the genetic integrity. Please don't offer the ponies titbits. It encourages them to approach people and cars which isn't always good for their well-being

Note: Be aware: part of this route is across open moorland, so a map and compass are needed – and clear weather conditions

---

From the car park walk back to the lane and turn right for about 100m. Cross the road and take the bridleway directing you up through the beech trees. This is Birch Cleave Wood, the highest beech woodland in the country at 350m above sea level. This path goes to Landacre via Pickedstones, the latter being where you are

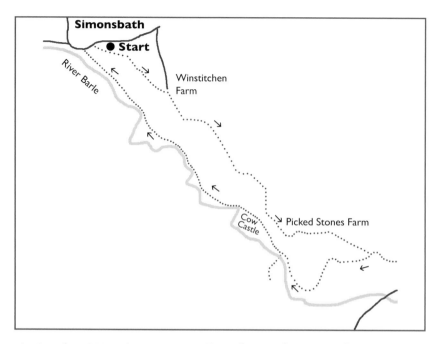

aiming for, 2½ miles away. Follow this path across the bottom of the woodland until you reach a three-way fingerpost. Turn left uphill for Pickedstones, you will see blue blobs from time to time which tell you you're on the right track.

As the path levels out another fingerpost points you to Landacre via Pickedstones, so follow this and keep your eyes open until you see a sign pointing you off the path and right through a gate. In the field walk ahead with the hedge on your left. At the field end pass through two gates in quick succession. You will find a small pond beyond the second gate. After the second gate bear right across the next field to gates which you can see in the hedge beneath a tree.

When you arrive at the gates take the left hand one of the two, which has a blue marker, then turn left to follow the boundary on your left. The land slopes away to your right with lovely views across the combes. You will be exploring the nearer valley later. At the end of this field continue in the same line through the next and you will reach a corrugated metal shed. Continue beyond here in the same direction and you will see the buildings of Winstitchen Farm ahead and to the left. When you reach the farm gate near the buildings turn right to walk away from the farm, the boundary on your left. Take a close look at this boundary as it's a traditional bank with an old laid hedge along the top, the young trees springing vertically from the horizontal branches which were laid along the top of the bank.

About 350m from the farm you will see another gate on your left with a blue blob. Turn left through it and walk ahead with the boundary of the field on your left. Beyond this field continue ahead through another two fields in the same direction. Eventually a conifer copse appears on the left. Continue past this with the trees on your left. You are descending now and the path becomes a track.

Exmoor farmland

View of Cow Castle & the Calf on the outward journey

You will see another fingerpost and blue markers directing you to bear right with the track a little way beyond the conifers.

Once you have gone right with the track you start to descend quite rapidly. Keep looking to your right across the valley and you will get a glimpse of the grassy mound of Cow Castle with its rampart – you will be over there later on the return journey. The track winds down to cross White Water, an idyllic spot to linger. After the river go through the gate and turn right to continue with the track. You start to ascend and Cow Castle can again be seen to your right, with the smaller 'Calf' visible beyond it.

The track leads you to a gate and into a field with a conifer plantation down to the right. Keep ahead and at the end of the field go left through a gate to follow the track past Pickedstones Farmhouse on your left. Beyond the farm the track leads past a barn on your right, join the tarmac farm drive and walk away from the farm. After about 300m this drive passes through a hedged boundary and shortly beyond this you'll find a bridleway fingerpost pointing you right off the drive and into a field. This tells you that you are heading for Landacre 2 miles and Withypool 3 miles. You're not actually going to either of these places but for the moment this is your route. Follow the direction given and walk through the field to the opposite boundary, the hedge is over to your right. In the far boundary you find a gate with a blue marker. This leads you onto open moorland.

A bridleway sign points you straight ahead here towards Withypool (ignore the arrows pointing left and right) and this lovely, airy route heading east straight across the moor is the way you need. Follow the clear track for ¾ mile, enjoying stunning views to the right, until you meet a three-way fingerpost (grid ref SS370818). You stand a very good chance in this area of seeing one of the herds of Exmoor ponies. When you reach the fingerpost turn sharp right – you are now heading towards Simonsbath via Cow Castle, 4 miles away on the Two Moors Way, denoted by an 'M' over a 'W'.

This new direction leads you gently downhill. Keep ahead and eventually you will see the medieval Landacre Bridge away down in the valley to your left. Enjoy this broad, grassy path as it eventually leads you to a gate nearly a mile from the point at which you joined the Two Moors Way. Beyond the gate continue on the clear track, the river is down to your left. After another gate continue, with rising ground to your right, the river still below to your left and a conifer plantation coming into view ahead. The path enters the trees on a lovely broad track. Keep with it for about ½ mile, admiring the densely mossy tree trunks in the boundary on your left, and resisting the temptation to go up into the conifers, for there lies darkness and no bridleway. When you reach a fork go left towards the river and just before you reach the water go right on a narrower path between the trees beside the water. This

Wheal Eliza

'Wheal' derives from the Cornish 'huel', which means a mine working. Originally called Wheal Maria, Wheal Eliza originated as a copper mine in 1845 before moving over to iron in 1854. The quantities of iron ore were disappointing and it closed in 1857 after three owners and six mine captains attempted to make it viable. The ruins that remain today are of the mine workshop and a store, which later became a shepherd's cottage, last occupied in 1952. Evidence suggests that first mining activities here may have existed as early as 1552. The site is infamous, however, as the scene where the body of 6-year-old Hannah Maria Burgess was located. Her father, John Burgess, murdered her because of a hostile relationship between his mistress and the little girl. In June 1858 he set out with the child stating that he was taking her to live with

her grandmother at Porlock Weir. Instead he killed her on the moors and dumped her body in the old shaft at the Wheal Eliza mine. Her body was uncovered some months after and William Henry Thornton, first incumbent of the new church of St Luke in Simonsbath, was instrumental in bringing the murderer to justice. John Burgess was later hanged on 4th January 1859 at Taunton.

quickly leads to an open, grassy area which is good for a picnic, but if you decide to sit on the inviting, flat stone mind the metal spikes which could prod the unwary sitter.

Beyond here you will see a footbridge on the left with a path leading to Blue Gate. You DON'T want this. Follow the Two Moors Way path signed Simonsbath 2¼ miles, to another little footbridge a few metres away after some stepping stones. Cross this smaller footbridge followed by a stile and follow the trodden path towards the grassy heights of Cow Castle just ahead of you, passing the Calf on your right as you approach it. A blue marker helps direct you here, leading you between Cow Castle and the Calf. Note the grassy path going up Cow Castle and, less faint-hearted walkers, although this may beckon it isn't actually a public footpath or access land. However, someone must occasionally struggle up the slope as years ago we found a retired wheelbarrow up there.

More biddable walkers should stick to the public footpath and walk anti-clockwise round Cow Castle. When you meet the stone wall keep going round with the Castle on your left and the wall on your right, following its line towards the river. This is the Barle.

When you meet the river turn right through a bridleway gate and follow the path with the river to your left and the wall to your right, don't be tempted to pass through the wall. As you go glance up to the hillside ahead. When we walked this route for the book we saw a herd of 23+ red deer up there, watching us. This path leads to one of Simone's favourite places, a lovely crescent of

Conifers beside the River Barle

ancient trees overhanging the river. Enjoy them from all angles, they are quite beautiful.

Follow the path beside the river. Towards the end of the crescent a blue marker directs you through a gap in the tree boundary (to avoid wet feet) so that you are now walking with the trees to your left and the river beyond them. After a few metres you are directed back through the trees to continue in the same direction along the path.

Keep with this path now as the river meanders in and out to your left. After a stretch of level walking the path leads up to a gate and you approach the ruined mine workings of Wheal Eliza. Beyond this the path bends away from the river to wind around the hill before you once more see the river on your left. Ahead of you along the valley you can see the beech woodland whence you started. Follow the path as it leads you into these trees, now on a lower path, and back to the lane at Simonsbath. From here retrace your steps to the car park.

Cheddar Gorge

This walk takes in some of the most astonishing scenery the West Country has to offer. It involves a couple of steep ascents to get above the gorge and care must be taken when near edges. The paths are good and clear but can be slippery so good boots are essential. The dramatic scenery is unrivalled in Somerset.

Map: OS Explorer 141 Cheddar Gorge and Mendip Hills West 1:25 000

Start point: Black Rock car park. No post code. Grid ref ST482545

Directions to start: Black Rock Nature Reserve is on the B3135 at the far end of the gorge from the village of Cheddar

Parking: There is an area to the side of the road where cars can be left

Distance: 4½ miles / 7.2km + further optional exploration of the National Trust Nature Reserves of Black Rock and Velvet Bottom

Refreshments: There are many places in Cheddar. A particularly nice lunch stop is Edelweiss: 01934 742347

Toilets: Signposted in Cheddar

Nearby places to stay: Many places advertise accommodation including Chedwell Cottage: 01934 743268 and Tor Farm, Nyland: 01934 743710

Nearby places of interest: There is some fascinating history to be found in the gorge including Cox's Cave and Gough's Cave: 01934 742343

Possible birds include: Collared dove, great tit, green woodpecker, jackdaw, kestrel, mallard, peregrine, pheasant, robin, wren

Authors' tip: We recommend allowing time to explore the area of Black Rock Nature Reserve and, adjacent to this, Velvet Bottom Nature Reserve. They provide an extra bit of good walking and bird watching through some very lovely scenery and are worth a 'there and back again' wander before returning to your car

---

From the car parking area cross the road and take the path (by the bus stop) uphill. This is the West Mendip Way towards Draycott and is a steep and rough path. As you climb you meet a bridleway marker post as a path comes up from the right. Continue uphill on the main path. Eventually you reach a gate with a yellow arrow. Pass through and continue ahead on the clear path. After about 100m you reach a fork. The West Mendip Way to Draycott goes

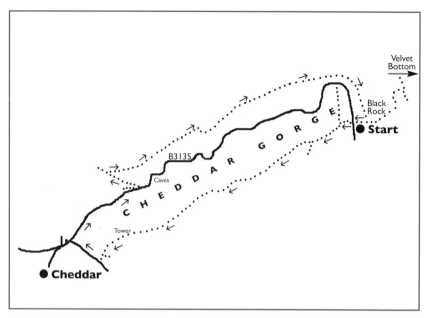

left but you need to keep right on the broad track which is closer to the gorge rim. You will soon see an arrow indicating that you are on the Gorge Walk.

At a tall, wooden gate pass through and continue. The path is clear as it winds its way above the gorge affording incredible views across the gorge and of the surrounding countryside including Glastonbury Tor, Brent Knoll and the distant coast. Take care, it's edgy in places. Eventually the path starts to drop and passes through more wooden gates to reach the area by the lookout tower at the top of Jacob's Ladder steps. These are privately owned tourist attractions. Your way lies on the bridleway to the left, heading into the trees. Keep going downhill, ignoring any lefts or rights, until you reach a drive. Turn right here heading down between houses. When you reach the lane turn right and follow it down until you meet the road which runs through the gorge. Turn right here, keeping an eye out for wayward traffic and somewhere for a cuppatea.

After refreshment continue to walk through the gorge until you pass Cox's Mill Hotel on the left and the millpond beyond it. After this you will find two footpaths on the left. One passes in front of the whitewashed Mark Hole Cottage and another, a few metres further along the road, passes behind the cottage. The one behind is the one you need.

Ignore the permissive path you soon meet on the right and continue until you reach another footpath going sharply right to take you behind Cufic Cottage and Cufic House. Take this and you soon emerge on a tarmac drive. Here immediately turn sharp right uphill on the path which leads away from houses with the gorge below to your right and the lookout at the top of Jacob's Ladder visible over to the right.

You climb to a kissing gate, pass through and continue on the path beyond up to another kissing gate, after which turn left. After

Fantastic views over the gorge

Two scenes of the magnificent rock formations

about 200m at an indistinct fork in the path keep left and continue through the trees – soon you will see a fence up on your left, the ground on your right slopes down into the gorge.

The path leads up to a stone wall with a stile by the top left corner. Over the stile turn sharply right back on yourself through a gap, as indicated by an arrow, to follow the wall, now on your right, to a gate with an arrow a few metres along. You are walking straight towards Glastonbury Tor in the distance. At the gate bear left on the trodden path towards the gorge. You soon reach another wall with a marker post nearby. Pause here and admire the amazing views around you. Glance behind for a view of Brent Knoll with the sea beyond.

Leave the post, following the wall on your right with the gorge beyond it. This is a well-trodden path and occasional arrows reassure you that you are following the Gorge Walk. Keep on the path with infrequent kissing gates, more-frequent goats, Exmoor ponies and great views into the gorge. Keep ahead above the gorge ignoring any options to right or left. The path eventually descends down steps to a wall with a big, stepped stile in front of you. The Gorge Walk goes right here but you need to leave it at this point and cross the stile, continuing with the path beyond it as it curves right to enter trees. You are now skirting the top end of the gorge. Cross a stile and continue. The path briefly emerges from trees before it re-enters woodland and eventually drops down to a broad crossing path by a gate.

From here you have the option which we would highly recommend. To explore the landscape of Black Rock go left on the clear path which will also lead you to a gate on the right into the Velvet Bottom reserve. These are beautiful spots for bird watching and picnics. Those not wishing to explore further should turn right at the bottom of the slope, following the track the short distance back to the car parking area.

Across the gorge

Cheddar

The area of Cheddar is awash with history, evidence of human occupation dating back millennia. The discovery in Gough's Cave of 'skull cups' is possible evidence of our ancestors' cannibalistic tendencies. The human skulls are fashioned as drinking vessels and are over 14,000 years old, and Britain's oldest, complete, human skeleton was  found here in the early 20thC. Cheddar Man, as he is dubbed, is thought to be over 7,000 years old. Cheddar Gorge is the largest (but not the deepest) gorge in the UK and is a designated Site of Special Scientific Interest. This area is home to the original Cheddar cheese which has been produced here since the Middle Ages and possibly even before that, when the humidity and temperature in the caves was found to be ideal for maturing the cheese. Today only one local Cheddar-making company exists.

Looking towards Black Rock Nature Reserve

Walk 8
Burrington Combe

This is a walk of cave entrances and ancient burial sites – which have quite dramatic stories in their own right. The route climbs up out of the combe past trickling brooks onto the open heights of Black Down. The paths are good, the ascents steady, the views magnificent.

Map:	OS Explorer 141 Cheddar Gorge and Mendip Hills West 1:25 000
Start point:	Car park. Post code BS40 7AT. Grid ref ST476588
Directions to start:	Burrington Combe is on the B3134 just south of the village of Burrington and west of the more sizeable village of Blagdon. The car park required is on the north side of the combe, just south of The Burrington Inn
Parking:	There is an area to the side of the road where cars can be left, next to the public toilets and just down the road from The Burrington Inn
Distance:	4¼ miles / 6.8km
Refreshments:	The Burrington Inn: 01761 462227
Toilets:	At the car park
Nearby places to stay:	Winston Manor Hotel: 01934 852348
Nearby places of interest:	Various attractions and caves open to the public in Cheddar Gorge: 01934 742343
Possible birds include:	Blackbird, buzzard, carrion crow, jackdaw, raven, song thrush, woodpigeon, wren
Authors' tip:	Although the caves on this route look enticing they are not part of the walk and we don't recommend exploration unless you are qualified and equipped for this and have, where necessary, relevant permission
Note:	**Be aware: part of this route is across open moorland, so a map and compass are needed – and clear weather conditions**

From the car park cross the road and take the trodden path running beside the road. The huge hulk of rock you pass is known as The Rock of Ages. This was, allegedly, the sheltering place of Reverend Toplady and the inspiration for the hymn of the same name which he wrote, but this theory has recently been refuted. Just after the rock, on the other side of the road, you will see the cave entrance to Aveline's Hole – see feature on page 56 and the authors' tip above.

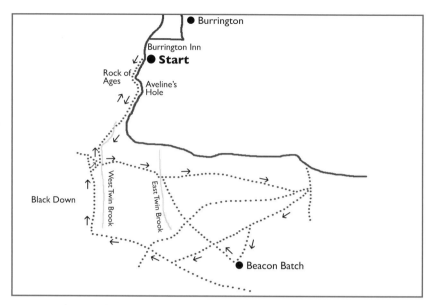

Follow the path beside the road as it leads through the gorge to eventually climb uphill away from the road. Follow it up, ignoring any turnings off it going back downhill. As it climbs it crosses and re-crosses West Twin Brook several times. Just before a flight of steps look to the right to see the entrance to Sidcot Swallet. Half way up the steps you will see a path going right, this is what you need but first ascend a little further to peer into the entrance to another cavern then go back down and follow the path beside the stream, crossing it again at a square water-filled construction.

The path emerges up out of the combe and climbs to meet a cross-path. Remember this point (*) at grid ref ST475581 as you will be back here later. Turn left along the path to reach a sharp left bend. Go round it. The path you are now on is called the Limestone Link. It bears right, stick with it and keep an eye open for grazing Exmoor ponies – there were many here when we passed through. The path occasionally veers around muddy bits but keep generally straight on with glorious views opening up across the combe to your left and the rising land of Black Down to your right.

Keep on the path as it takes a sharp left turn over East Twin Brook – a lovely glade of successive, shallow waterfalls. Beyond the stream follow the path ignoring rights or lefts off it until you meet a fingerpost (grid ref ST490577) ¾ mile from East Twin Brook. From here ignore the bridleway going right (south) from the post and take the uphill path going south-west obliquely back on yourself. Your way is a steady drag up to Beacon Batch, the highest point in the Mendips at 325 feet but the puff is rewarded by views ahead, to the right and behind. The path starts to flatten out and veers right at a broad sweep. Along here look out for a left turn at grid ref ST485475 – take this left path as it leads you up to the trig point, passing a little cairn on the right.

The trig point is on a Bronze Age burial mound of which there are several in the vicinity. When we were there two hardy men were labouring in sub-zero conditions to preserve the ground around the trig with a technique known as 'stone pitching'. The passage

Rock of Ages

of many feet, hooves and bike tyres takes its toll on this ancient site as travellers come to observe the less ancient 18thC monument of the trig point. When you reach the trig point take the first path to the right away from it heading northwest back to the track you left earlier. You reach this track at a crossing of ways – go left, now heading south west, until, in about 300m you meet an oblique crossing track (ST481572). Turn right along here and at a meeting of ways in another 300m (ST478572), with a fork ahead of

you, take the right hand path heading slightly north of west. Ignore the first path right after just over 100m and 350m from the fork you see a broad downhill path on the right (ST475573). Go right here, heading north.

Ignore lefts and right and walk towards the gorge on this main path, keeping right at a fork until, 900m from turning onto this path, you see a right hand path (ST474579) heading distinctly down towards the trees in Burrington Combe. See photo above to aid your direction! This path leads down for about 100m to a familiar crossways (*). Go straight across and retrace your steps, crossing West Twin Brook a few times on your way back to the road and your car. As you walk through the combe look out for the attractive goats who graze the area.

Aveline's Hole

This cave is famous for being the earliest scientifically dated cemetery in the British Isles. It was accidentally rediscovered in 1797 by two men digging for a rabbit. Excavations followed leading to reports of 70–100 skeletons lying side by side within. When the University of Bristol Spelaeological Society (UBSS) returned to excavate the site in 1914 only the remains  of 21 individuals were found. These were subsequently removed and housed in a Bristol Museum, only to be largely destroyed during a WWII bombing raid in 1940. In 2003 scientific tests on the few remaining bone fragments revealed them to be around 10,200–10,400 years old. As well as human remains there have also been a series of inscribed crosses found on the cave wall dating back to the early Mesolithic period (post ice age).

Cadbury Castle & Corton Denham

This fabulous walk has the drama of high hills, history, stunning views and one of our favourite hostelries – The Queen's Arms at Corton Denham. This lovely pub has a sign outside welcoming muddy boots and dogs, which is the kind of welcome we need. Despite the fact that there are no craggy gorges this route is awesome. The two very pretty villages of South Cadbury and Corton Denham are an added appeal.

Map:	OS Explorer 129 Yeovil & Sherborne 1:25 000
Start point:	Cadbury Castle car park, just on the edge of South Cadbury village. Post code BA22 7HA. Grid ref: ST632253
Directions to start:	South Cadbury is just off the A303 near Sparkford
Parking:	In designated car park, see above. There is also a cycle rack here for the more-energetic arrivals, lots of nice daffs in spring and the lovely welcoming sounds of exuberant free range chickens at the adjacent farm
Distance:	7½ miles / 12km
Refreshments:	The Camelot, South Cadbury: 01963 440448; The Queen's Arms, Corton Denham: 01963 220317
Toilets:	None en route
Nearby places to stay:	The Queen's Arms, Corton Denham: 01963 220317
Nearby places of interest:	Fleet Air Arm Museum, Ilchester: 01935 840565; Haynes International Motor Museum, Sparkford: 01963 440804; Sherborne Abbey: 01935 812452
Possible birds include:	Blackbird, blue tit, buzzard, chaffinch, chickens (!), great spotted woodpecker, great tit, green woodpecker, house sparrow, jackdaw, kestrel, partridge, pheasant, robin, rook, siskin, woodpigeon, yellowhammer
Authors' tip:	Although the footpath doesn't actually go up onto the Beacon on the return trip from Corton Denham, this is access land and the effort to climb the hill is well-rewarded by the indescribably good views. It's really not to be missed if you can summon the energy after the excellent food in The Queen's Arms

From the car park turn right along the lane for a few metres to Castle Lane. Go left up here, it quickly becomes a footpath and leads you up onto the hill fort of Cadbury Castle, negotiating a kissing gate for the very slim en route. It was tricky to get the

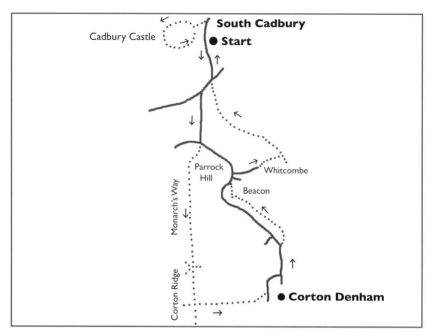

rucksacks through! Once you're on the hill fort take time to drink in the fabulous views and explore the ramparts, the footpath goes right the way round. It's a beautiful spot with a board on the summit detailing the surrounding area.

From the castle return the way you came up, turn right on the lane and continue along it, passing the car park on your left. Follow this lane (Church Road) past Crangs Lane until you reach the turning on the left, ½ mile from the car park, for Corton Denham and Sherborne. This is also part of Sustrans Route 26. Glance back as you go along this lane to the heights of the hill fort.

When you reach a T-junction go left and immediately right on the bridleway. There is a wooden post here showing you are on the Monarch's Way, a 610 mile path following the escape route taken by Charles II in 1651 after the Battle of Worcester. This path is also part of the Macmillan Way. After a short stretch of track go through the gate and bear right. You are climbing Parrock Hill. Keep ascending, admiring the views around and behind you – the hill fort is over your right shoulder, the woodland of Hicknoll Hanging over your left and the villages of Sutton Montis and Weston Bampfylde are below to your right.

The path begins to level out, with rising land still to your left and sweeping views to your right. Pass through a gate and continue straight ahead in a southerly direction. As you walk, to your left you see the heights of the Beacon on Corton Hill, which is where you'll be later.

Continue in the same direction, passing through large fields and another two gates. You eventually reach a gate on the left at the end of a field with a collection of arrows on the far side. This is 1¼ miles from leaving the lane. Pass through this left hand gate to find a meeting of ways. Turn right and go through another gate to

From Cadbury Castle   *Corton Denham church*

continue through the next field in the same direction as before with the hedge on your left. This is still the Monarch's / Macmillan Way, this section of path being known as Corton Ridge.

After about 500m through this field look out for a gap in the hedge on your left with some steps leading up to a kissing gate. Go through here and straight across the next three fields towards Corton Denham, nestling below the hillside. The final stile leads you onto a track. Head straight down here as far as a residential lane. This is Middle Ridge Lane. Turn left, following it as it then bends right. When you reach the main lane with the church in front of you, turn right to seek the embrace of The Queen's Arms.

Leave her and turn left along the lane, passing Middle Ridge Lane from which you emerged earlier and continuing uphill until the road bends left and drops. At this bend you will see a track heading right with a post denoting that you are heading for Corton Hill and Whitcombe (spellings of the latter vary from post to post!). Follow this track enjoying the views to your left as you climb. At a fork keep ahead, ignoring the right turn and keeping the fence on your left. Soon you reach a gate. Beyond here continue ahead with the fence still to your left. Beacon Hill is looming above you at 196m above sea level. The footpath follows the fence but as this is access land you can go up to explore the Beacon if you wish – it's unmissably worth it and from there you will be looking down on your earlier ascent of Cadbury Castle.

The footpath below the hill meets two gates, one low down and one higher up to the right, and it's this higher one you want, continuing to walk in the same direction below the Beacon (unless you're up on it, in which case you need to descend to this path when you've had enough of the wild heights). Follow the path beside the fence as it goes left and eventually passes through the tree boundary. Beyond this keep on with the tree boundary to your right and the path will lead to the corner of the field with a stile onto the lane.

Turn right along the lane and within 100m you meet two right turns in quick succession. Take the second, signposted for Whitcombe Farm. At the end of the lane pass the barn conversions on the left and keep straight ahead, entering a farmyard. Look for the track beyond the farm buildings on the far side of the yard and take this – you will see a footpath sign here telling you that this is a restricted byway. To your left from here you can see Cadbury Castle. Within 100m a track veers right with a ramshackle sign pointing you along it. Follow this and within another 100m keep left (straight on) at the fork. The path soon emerges to lead you up through a field. After about 200m you meet a fence and gate ahead. Turn left, staying in the same field, to walk beside the fence on your right. You're heading across the top of the field now towards

Parrock Hill and Cadbury Castle from The Beacon

Cadbury Castle

With one of the longest records of occupation of any hill fort in the country, Cadbury Castle has had human presence since several thousand years BC. Standing on this ancient site, cast your mind back through the millennia to imagine the changes it's seen: changes in language, government, farming practices, climate, the way people dress and eat, their average height and life expectancy.... Neolithic pottery has been found here and the tales told by successive excavations from 1890 onwards indicate that a Bronze Age settlement was superseded by a more robust Iron Age fort which later drew the aggressive attentions of the Romans and the population dispersed from the hill. By 500AD it was once again a substantial fort. During the 11thC, when the Vikings were threatening, it was used as a well-defended administrative centre and a Saxon mint was established for a brief time. Today, its commanding position affords glorious views and wonderful walking along the ramparts (see inset pic) with little indication of its turbulent history.

the mound of Cadbury Castle with rising ground to your right. The field you are crossing is the site of the medieval village of Whitcombe – only undulations remain since it was abandoned in the 17thC.

At the end of this field continue straight ahead through the next field – an arrow directs – with the boundary to your right. At the end cross the stile on the right and then turn left to walk across another field (a grassy path was provided at the time of writing) towards a house. Look around you – you are within a 'bowl' of hills. At the end of the field cross the plank bridge under an oak, followed by a stile. After this walk up the next small field to another stile onto the lane. Turn right along the lane, passing Crangs Lane on your right, and soon you're back at the car park.

Walk 10

Blagdon Hill

Although not as dramatic as other walks in this book we feel the Blackdown Hills are worthy of inclusion for their tranquil beauty. Aside from one steepish, muddy ascent this fairly straightforward ramble affords wonderful views and, unusually, a choice of three pubs en route.

Map: OS Explorer 128 Taunton & Blackdown Hills 1:25 000

Start point: At a stile opposite The Blagdon Inn in the village of Blagdon Hill. Post code TA3 7SG. Grid ref: ST211183

Directions to start: The village of Blagdon Hill is 4 miles south of Taunton

Parking: There is a small parking area at the start point and another between The Blagdon Inn and the Post Office. Otherwise, use of either pub may enable you to gain permission to park for an extended period – please ask

Distance: 5 miles / 8 km

Refreshments: The Blagdon Inn, Blagdon Hill: 01823 421296; Holman Clavel Inn, Culmhead: 01823 421432; The Lamb & Flag, Blagdon Hill: 01823 421736; The Merry Harriers, Clayhidon: 01823 421270; The Half Moon Inn, Clayhidon: 01823 680291

Toilets: None en route

Nearby places to stay: Culmhead House, Culmhead: 01823 421073; Holly Bush Park (B&B, Caravan & Camping), Culmhead: 01823 421515

Nearby places of interest: Sheppy's Cider, Bradford-on-Tone: 01823 461233; Somerset Cricket Museum, Taunton: 01823 275893

Possible birds include: Blackbird, blue tit, buzzard, carrion crow, chaffinch, great tit, house sparrow, magpie, mallard, pheasant, woodpigeon, wren

Authors' tip: For stunning views over the Vale of Taunton take a short drive eastwards to Staple Hill car park at OS Grid ref: ST247159. From here we recommend the Viewpoint Walk (0.6 mile / 1 km). On a really clear day the views along here can stretch beyond the Quantocks and the Bristol Channel to the coast of Wales

---

Cross over a stile adjacent to a public phone box and opposite the Blagdon Inn. Take this public footpath keeping the hedge on your left to the far corner of the field. Pass through a kissing gate and emerge onto a lane. Turn left here and then almost immediately right up Quarry Lane. This leads into the drive of Quarry House,

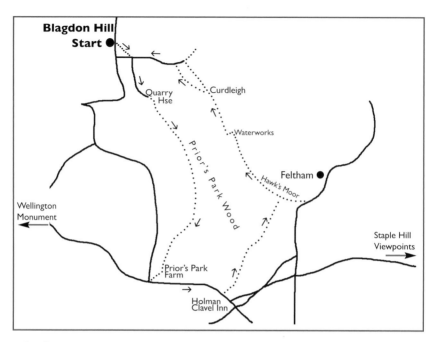

which you pass on your left. There are other buildings on your right too – keep straight ahead beyond these and emerge into a yard with a stile in the left hand corner. There are sumptuous views away to your left here.

Cross the stile and keep ahead with a fence on your left. Before long you're walking between hedges and approaching woodland to your left. This narrow section soon passes through a gateway with a stile adjacent to it. Continue straight ahead – you now have the woodland directly to your left and a bank to your right.

In approximately 40m the path entices you into the woodland. Accept the offer and keep ahead on a clear track. After some distance ignore a broad left option and continue ahead on the path as it climbs steadily up through the woods. It does get wet along here and at one point, particularly in the rainy season, the path could have you wading through a shallow stream. You continue your ascent to emerge from the woodland at a gate, which shows on the reverse that you have just left behind a restricted byway.

Beyond the gate follow the path ahead as it curves to the left with a field sloping up to the right. You soon meet another gate on the left which you pass through. To the left you can peek over the hedge boundary towards Hawk's Moor and North Down Plantation. Continue forward on a clear path which is fenced off within a field. As you head up to the buildings of Prior's Park Farm the views begin to open up to your left and behind you.

Proceed through the gate just in front of the farm buildings and turn right. Keep between the farm buildings with the house on your left and barns to your right. Leave the buildings as you progress along the drive to a lane where you turn left. Tread with caution along this relatively busy road whilst admiring views to the left over the aforementioned Hawk's Moor and North Down

View of the hills from the top of Quarry Lane

View over the Vale of Taunton above Blagdon Hill

Plantation. The lure of the Holman Clavel Inn awaits you so don't get too despondent whilst treading tarmac underfoot over this short distance. You'll notice a footpath off to the left opposite the Holly Bush Park caravan park. This is your return route. However, for research purposes, we headed on for refreshment at the Holman Clavel Inn.

Return to the footpath off the road, head down the track and across a stile. You are now entering Forestry Commission woodland. Keep ahead on the broad path with woodland to your right and views to your left. At the time of writing much of this woodland had opened out considerably due to logging, but the footpath is, and should remain, signposted.

Approximately 200m from the stile go right at a distinct fork with a public footpath sign pinned to a tree for guidance. As you proceed there are lovely views to the left. In a further 300m you approach another fork. Keep right here and continue as the path climbs slightly and then swings left. You pass by a stout bench and soon afterwards the path begins to get narrower. Views over the village of Blagdon Hill and beyond will soon open up to your left.

The narrow path begins to wind left and right as it drops downhill to cross a stream. There are a series of small tumbling waterfalls here which made for a timely thirst-quenching oasis for our over-parched pooch.

Beyond the stream the path ascends and winds it way through trees to emerge at a T-junction of paths. There are lovely views from here to the village of Feltham and beyond. Turn left and keep going on a trodden path as it eventually drops down to another stream. Cross this and continue along the path with the water to your right.

The Blackdown Hills

The Blackdown Hills are often overlooked by visitors as they pass on the M5 motorway in their haste to reach their holiday destinations. This beautiful range of hills, which sit either side of the Somerset/Devon border, are far more deserving of exploration. They cover 143 square miles and have seen human occupation since the Iron Age. Staple Hill, a Marilyn (see page 79), is the highest point, standing at 315m above sea level. The Wellington Monument (see pic insert) was erected in the 19thC to honour the Duke of Wellington following his victory at Waterloo. Work began on the obelisk in 1817 but sadly, due to a lack of funds, it wasn't completed until 1892 (40 years after the death of the Iron Duke). It stands proudly on the Blackdowns just south of Wellington and heralds far-reaching views over Somerset. The Blackdowns were designated an Area of Outstanding Natural Beauty in 1991.

The stream leads you to an enclosed waterworks area. Follow the footpath as it passes to the left adjacent to the perimeter fence until you reach the entrance gates. At this point turn left along a forestry track away from the gates. Follow this as, in 50m, it swings to the right. Ignore the left turn here and be guided by the footpath arrow which directs you. Keep following this track as it passes through trees echoing with the babbling sounds of streams.

You eventually reach a gate which you pass through and continue ahead towards farm buildings at Curdleigh. Go through another gate and turn left along a fairly scenic tarmac drive and, as a road comes in to meet you from the right, bear left and continue ahead. Pass Quarry Lane from earlier on and either turn right via the footpath to retrace your steps across the field back to your car or venture ahead for a pint at the Lamb & Flag.

Enjoying the scene from Staple Hill viewpoint (see authors' tip page 63)

Walk 11
County Gate, Exmoor

Although this walk is the shortest in the book it has lots of gems in one small package: open moorland, verdant combes, a lovely waterfall, big coastline and striking views. There is quite a steep climb towards the end but this is soon rewarded by refreshment in the café at County Gate.

Map: OS Outdoor Leisure 9, Exmoor 1:25 000

Start point: Car park at County Gate. Post code EX35 6NY. Grid ref SS793486

Directions to start: County Gate is situated between Lynmouth and Porlock on the A39

Parking: Car park at County Gate (as above)

Distance: 3¾ miles / 6 km

Refreshments: There is a café at the Visitor Centre, County Gate

Toilets: In the car park at County Gate

Nearby places to stay: Blue Ball Inn, Countisbury: 01598 741263 (very dog friendly); The Gables, Porlock: 01643 863432

Nearby places of interest: Exmoor Coast Boat Trips, Lynmouth: 01598 753207. Glen Lyn Gorge, Lynmouth: 01598 753207

Possible birds include: Blackbird, blue tit, carrion crow, chaffinch, great tit, green woodpecker, magpie, pheasant, raven, skylark, woodpigeon, wren

Authors' tip: County Gate is also a good starting point for exploring the Glenthorne Estate where there are steep trails to a pinetum and stony beach

Note: Be aware: part of this route is across open moorland, so a map and compass are useful – and clear weather conditions

---

Enjoy the car park. Seek out the 'view indicator' in its far corner and savour this spot before starting the walk. From the car park cross the road and pick up the blue-arrowed bridleway signed for Broomstreet. This is a nice clear track with fabulous views across the moorland. Soon you reach a fingerpost at which you continue ahead on the bridleway. Less than 100m further the path forks. Left is to the viewpoint at Sugarloaf, but our way lies straight on. (You will return on the path from Sugarloaf later.) Three quarters of a mile after leaving the lane you reach Yenworthy Lodge. Beyond the house cross over their drive and

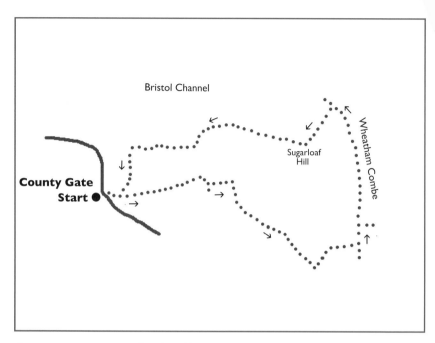

then continue on the bridleway opposite, still signposted for Broomstreet Farm and now also Oareford.

From the driveway the path ascends to a gate. After this keep on the clear track, there are boundaries to your left and right. When you reach the end of the right hand fence keep ahead on the trodden path, slightly uphill. Soon the path levels out through the field, stay in this field and follow the wall and fence on the left, with an occasional blue bridleway marker. This is a lovely stretch of walking. You reach a crossing fence which, at the time of writing, was brand new with no markers. Pass through the field gate and continue in the same direction alongside the wall until the track starts to descend, still close to the wall (admire its lovely mossy roundness and beech topping).

At the end of the wall follow it round to the left and then bear right again to continue to follow the boundary. The wall leads you to another fingerpost directing you through a gate on the left, still towards Broomstreet. Follow this downhill, boundary to your right, with good views ahead and to Sugarloaf Hill. When you reach another fingerpost carry on ahead, now on the coast path to Lynmouth (the bridleway goes off here), you are heading into Wheatham Combe. At the next fingerpost go right through a gap in the boundary into this lovely, verdant area. The stream is down to the left. This is a good place for a picnic and the trodden path leads you clearly through the combe and down to a fingerpost. Beyond this descend steps to cross the stream, climbing up out of the combe on the far side with the stream now on your right. Follow the path to a gate then continue beyond it, there are trees down to your right with glimpses of the sea through them.

Eventually you leave the trees behind and good coastal views open up. As you round the headland, with the sea to your right, spare a glance back along the glorious coastline. Soon you reach a three-

Gorse and Glenthorne

En route back to County Gate

way fingerpost at Guildhall Corner. Go left here on the permissive path, signed for Sugarloaf and County Gate. This is quite a climb up beside the left hand boundary but fear not, there will be a bench waiting for you at the top! Follow the path as it veers right away from the boundary and then climbs less steeply. There are excellent views to the right to take your mind off the puff. At the top of the hill you will find yourself looking over a wall to Yenworthy Lodge on the hillside beyond. Turn right to follow the wall to a gap with a yellow footpath marker on the stones, sampling the bench if you wish.

Beyond the gap drink in the views along the N. Devon coastline and then turn left towards County Gate, tottering steeply downhill beside the wall to a fingerpost by a stream. A diversion of about 50m is worthwhile here – follow the path to the right, with the stream to your left until you find a delightful waterfall (see first colour plate), you'll hear it before you see it. Return to the fingerpost, cross the stream and follow the trodden path beyond, you will see occasional yellow footpath markers along the way. The path goes up the hillside, fence up to the left, stream down to the right and lovely views ahead as you climb. The path goes up to a gate, go through and continue beyond it now with the fence on you right. Soon you have spectacular views down to the house of Glenthorne in its prime position at the bottom of a combe above the sea – setting for Christopher Ondaatje's story *The Glenthorne Cat.*

Keep following the fence on your right, it eventually bends right and leads up to a stile. Continue in the same direction beyond here along the fence, until it goes steeply up to another stile on the right in front of a gate. Cross the stile and now follow the boundary on your left, a fingerpost shows you are still en route for County Gate. There are good combe and sea views down to your right. The path winds inland along the top of the combe. At a fingerpost go right along the track to another fingerpost. Turn right here and now you are retracing your steps the short distance to County Gate.

County Gate

Reopened as a visitor centre in 2010, the former gatehouse at County Gate now comes complete with a tearoom and garden. This 18thC Grade II listed cottage was acquired by the Exmoor National Park Authority in 1977, when nearby Cosgate Hill was purchased. Previously, there had been an information caravan based in the car  park. This, however, overturned in a storm, spilling its contents of literature across the moor. The centre moved to the gatehouse in 1980. Situated roughly half way between Porlock and Lynmouth it also served as a staging post for horse-drawn coaches until the 1920s. The actual 'Gate', which spanned the road, is long gone, but its stone posts remain. At over 330m above sea level the location of the centre on the Somerset/Devon border is undeniably breathtaking. To the south it overlooks the valley of the East Lyn river, whilst to the north the moor descends sharply to the Bristol Channel with, on a clear day, the coast of Wales beyond. County Gate lies within easy proximity of both the South West Coast Path and the Two Moors Way and is justifiably popular with walkers.

Walk 12
Cothelstone & the South Quantocks

Although this walk is very high it starts at an elevated point and the only really stiff climb is ascending from the lane after Durborough Farm. This lovely route affords views of the Blackdown, Mendip and Brendon Hills, Dartmoor and Exmoor, across the sea to the islands of Flat Holm and Steep Holm and beyond these to Wales.

Map: OS Explorer 140 Quantock Hills and Bridgwater 1:25 000

Start point: Lydeard Hill car park. No post code. Grid ref ST180338

Directions to start: Cothelstone village is north east of Bishops Lydeard off the A358. Continue through Cothelstone to a junction called Park End, turn left here to a crossroads called Birches Corner and Lydeard Hill car park is signed from here

Parking: Lydeard Hill car park, see above

Distance: 5¾ miles / 9.25km or longer option 7¾ miles / 12.5km

Refreshments: The Bird in Hand, Bishops Lydeard: 01823 432090; Blue Ball Inn, Triscombe: 01984 618242; The Rising Sun, West Bagborough: 01823 432575

Toilets: None en route

Nearby places to stay: Farrington Guest House: 01823 433087; The Mount, Bishops Lydeard: 01823 431897; Wayside House, West Bagborough: 01823 430108; West View, Bishops Lydeard: 01823 432223

Nearby places of interest: West Somerset Railway: 01643 704996

Possible birds include: Blue tit, buzzard, chaffinch, chiffchaff, coal tit, Dartford warbler, great tit, long-tailed tit, mallard, pheasant, raven, robin, skylark

Authors' tip: Although the longer option requires you to retrace your steps once you've visited Cothelstone Hill, the views are so tremendous from the top that we would recommend you do this

Note: Be aware: part of this route is across open moorland, so a map and compass are needed – and clear weather conditions

---

If you get no further than the car park today it will still be a good trip because, if conditions are clear, the views are magnificent. Select a bench! In the distance, in a south-westish direction, you can see the Wellington Monument (see page 67).

Leave the car park through the gate opposite the cattle grid over which you entered. This is signed for Lydeard Hill and beyond the

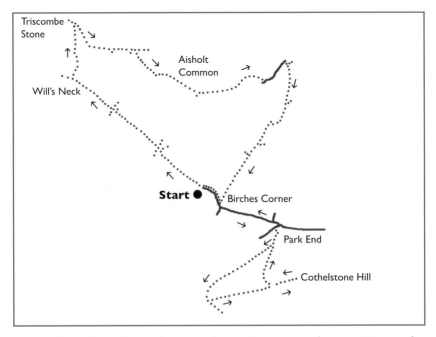

gate a broad track leads you ahead, ignoring the smaller paths leading right up onto the hill. Enjoy the views to your left and just over half a mile from the car park the path reaches a gate where options lead off in various directions. Go through the gates and continue in the same direction as before. There is now woodland to your left and the view opens up to your right – soon you get a glimpse of the sea at Bridgwater Bay beyond a conifer plantation.

At a fork in the path keep ahead in the same direction as indicated by a yellow arrow. The trees which have accompanied you on the left drift away and you are soon crossing open heathland. Keep straight ahead on a broad path uphill ignoring any lefts or rights until you reach the trig point at Will's Neck (a corruption of Wealas Nek, meaning 'Ridge of the Britons'). At 386m you are now on the highest point in the Quantocks – a good place to remember you have a hip flask. Views from here are magnificent on a clear day. To the north, at the mouth of the River Severn as it emerges into the Bristol Channel, are the islands of Steep Holm and Flat Holm (with its lighthouse). Beyond the islands the coast of Wales is visible. On this side of the water you will see the edifice of Hinkley Point nuclear power station. Continue your view around clockwise to take in the Mendip, Blackdown and Brendon Hills. Looking west along the coast is Minehead and the prominent white building there is Butlins!

From the trig point continue in the same direction along a clear path. This is all the Macmillan Way West though there is no sign to denote this. The track is an ancient Drove Road, used for centuries by farmers and traders. Stay on the main path ignoring any others and descend for about 200m until you meet a cross-ways of paths – keep a sharp eye out for this. Turn right along here, dropping down towards the distant landmark of Hinkley Point (don't worry – it's a long way off and you're not going there). Keep straight ahead downhill as other paths veer off. Away to your left you will see notices advising you to keep away from Triscombe Quarry, the stone from which was used to build one of the runways at Heathrow. At the bottom of the hill you find an open area with stile and gates. A brief diversion through these gates is a good idea to visit the Bronze Age Triscombe Stone, an ancient waymarker, in the area beyond. He isn't very big and likes to meet people. Return through the gates to the open area and continue ahead following the path through the edge of the woodland, keeping the boundary bank and wall of the wood to your left. The trees beyond this boundary are conifers but the path is passing through deciduous trees at the margin of the wood.

Follow this path, with its occasional bends, ignoring any paths off it until you have gone almost ¾ mile from the gates and stile. At this point you pass through a gap in another old wall running away from the one you have been following. Immediately after the gap you will see options on paths. Turn right and head downhill

View from Muchcare Wood

with this 'new' wall now on your right, the path you need runs down next to the wall. There are fabulous views from here to enjoy. Aisholt Common is to your left. Listen out for the cronk of ravens.

The path drops into the valley and bends occasionally, follow it, keeping the wall/bank boundary to your right and ignoring any paths off. Eventually you enter woodland and at the bottom of the hill the path bears left, with a stream to your right – which may dry up in summer. This is a lovely stretch of walking on a broad woodland path. In early spring the area is carpeted with violets and wood sorrel.

The trees thin out and there is an open field to your left. The stony path continues ahead (it can be a bit wet through here) and eventually emerges through a gate by Durborough Farm. Turn left along the lane, passing some idyllic thatched cottages and a pond.

In the early part of the year the snowdrops along here are beautiful – admire them but please don't pick them. A few hundred metres along the lane, opposite a cottage called Holcombe, you will find a ford on your right crossing the stream and a fingerpost beyond directing you through a gate and onto a 'restricted byway'.

Go up a short slope and when you see another gate and path bearing left don't follow this but stay on the main path as it swings sharply right to go steeply uphill. This is the toughest part of the walk but it's a lovely, deep track which feels very ancient. Just over ½ mile from the ford you meet a crossing path, go right here, still slightly uphill. The route takes a few bends but stay on the main path. After a sharp right followed by a sharp left the view opens up on the left – at this point you have woodland on your right with the curious name of Muchcare. At the brow of the hill you meet a footpath going off to the left. Ignore this and keep ahead with the woodland still to your right. As you walk up this path look left behind you to the town of Bridgwater in the distance.

When you reach a lane those less energetic can now turn right back to the car park along the permitted bridleway beside the lane. However, we would highly recommend turning left here to take in the spectacular views that await you atop Cothelstone Hill. For those who are on this longer option, keep straight ahead at Birches Corner on the road to Bishops Lydeard and Bridgwater. This road is not overly busy but as you are following it for about half a mile keep a sharp lookout for traffic. Even though you have tarmac underfoot this is another portion of the Macmillan Way West. Keep on this road until you reach a T-junction at Park End where you turn right heading towards Cothelstone and Bishops Lydeard.

After approximately 50m you'll see a bridleway gate on the left into the trees. Take this and after a few metres you'll be faced with

The Somerset Marilyns

Will's Neck is one of the Somerset Marilyns, a Marilyn being a hill with a relative height of at least 150m. Relative height is an indication of prominence in relation to the surrounding ground level as opposed to height above sea level (which is usually used for measuring hills and mountains). In some ways relative height gives a clearer idea of what you are about

to climb. Other Somerset Marilyns are Dunkery and Selworthy Beacons and Periton Hill. There are almost 180 English Marilyns listed although this list can change as systems of measurement become more refined.

three possible routes. Take the path heading right. It can be quite muddy through here after heavy rain. You are now walking through the bottom of the woodland and the lane is just down to your right. Stick with it as it bends right and starts to go uphill.

Keep on this track and as it begins to descend you'll notice another track off to the left going uphill. Take this and head up until you see an option to swing right uphill on a narrow path to a crossing path at a fence. Turn right here keeping the fence and rising land to your left. After a while the path bears left and you'll soon see a post with an arrow on the far side. At this point turn left to a gate with another arrow and continue to the summit of Cothelstone Hill passing a fence-encircled tumulus and further on a wooden bench dedicated to Bob Bedingfield, a supporter of the Quantocks.

At the top the 360° panorama from 332m above sea level makes all the effort worthwhile – believe us!

Retrace your steps to the tumulus where there is a footpath off to the right (north) at grid ref ST187326. Head downhill on this path and pass through a kissing gate. Beyond this there is a crossing path where you turn right. When the path forks there is a post with an arrow pointing you right. Rebel here and go left (this is all access land anyhow so don't worry). You'll soon see the gate in front of you through which you originally entered the woods.

Emerge through the gate onto the road and turn right to retrace your steps back to Park End. Here turn left passing Park End Lodge on the way back to Birches Corner. Once here keep ahead until you reach the point where you emerged from the track onto the lane earlier. Rather than walking along the lane to the car park join the permitted bridleway that runs through the woodland running parallel to the lane. It emerges at the car park.

On Cothelstone Hill – Bob Bedingfield's bench